HANDS-ON
Science

Forces and Motion

John Graham

Illustrations by David Le Jars

KINGFISHER
Kingfisher Publications Plc
New Penderel House,
283–288 High Holborn,
London WC1V 7HZ
www.kingfisherpub.com

Produced for Kingfisher by PAGE*One*
Cairn House, Elgiva Lane, Chesham
Buckinghamshire HP5 2JD

For PAGE*One*
Creative Director Bob Gordon
Project Editor Miriam Richardson
Designers Monica Bratt, Tim Stansfield

Illustrator David Le Jars

For Kingfisher
Managing Editor Clive Wilson
Production Controller Jacquie Horner
DTP Co-ordinator Nicky Studdart

First published by Kingfisher Publications Plc 2001
10 9 8 7 6 5 4 3 2 1
TS/0504/TIMS/GRS/150 MA/F

A CIP catalogue record for this book is available from
the British Library

ISBN 0 7534 0272 6

Printed in China

Introduction and safety tips
◆ 4 ◆

Measuring forces
◆ 6 ◆

Squeezing and twisting
◆ 8 ◆

Gravity
◆ 10 ◆

Balancing
◆ 12 ◆

CONTENTS

Pressure
♦ 14 ♦

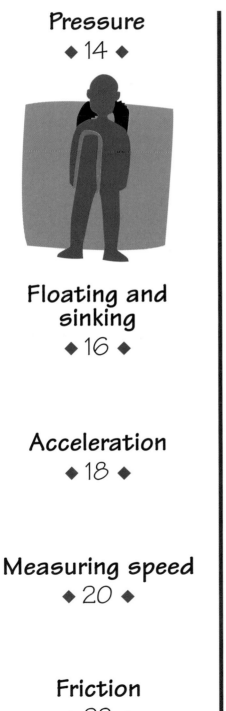

Floating and
sinking
♦ 16 ♦

Acceleration
♦ 18 ♦

Measuring speed
♦ 20 ♦

Friction
♦ 22 ♦

Air and water
resistance
♦ 24 ♦

Floating in air
♦ 26 ♦

Flight
♦ 28 ♦

Force magnifiers
♦ 30 ♦

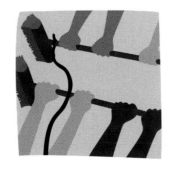

Gears
♦ 32 ♦

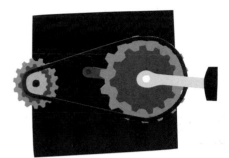

Circular motion
♦ 34 ♦

Starting and
stopping
♦ 36 ♦

Glossary
♦ 38 ♦

Index
♦ 40 ♦

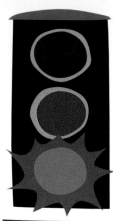

Getting started

Have you ever wondered why things move the way they do? What makes them start moving? Why do things fall when you drop them? Why is swimming so much harder than walking? You will discover answers to these questions, and many others, in this book. It is packed full of experiments to try out at home or at school, which will help you to understand forces and motion.

Feel the force

Every time you ride a bike, turn the door handle or even just move your arm, you are using forces. They are the invisible pushes and pulls that make everything happen.

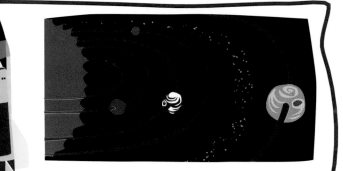

Athletes, dancers, racing drivers and builders all need to understand about forces. Every machine, from a playground see-saw to a space shuttle, relies on forces to work. From the tiny forces that hold atoms together to the huge forces that keep the planets going round the Sun, forces really are everywhere!

What you need

You can find most of the things you need for the activities in this book around your house or garage. If you do not happen to have exactly the item shown in the picture, you can probably use something similar that will do the same job. You may well find that you can improve on some of the ideas here. Improvisation is part of the fun of doing experiments!

Most of the activities use empty containers. Start saving plastic bottles, tubs and cartons. You never know what will come in handy!

Your experiments are more likely to be successful if you work carefully and tidy up as you go along.

Warning

Read through all the steps for an activity before you start. Then work through them steadily – rushing or getting carried away could cause an accident. A pair of scissors or a hammer could cause serious injury. Ask an adult for help. Have fun, but work safely!

Take special care when using glue. Make sure you are using the right sort. Follow the instructions carefully and pay attention to any safety warnings. If in doubt, ask an adult.

Out of doors, stay away from traffic, open water, overhead power lines or other hazards. Make sure a responsible adult knows where you are and what you are doing.

Clock symbol

The clock symbol at the start of each experiment shows you approximately how many minutes the activity should take. All the experiments take between 5 and 30 minutes. If you are using glue, allow extra time for drying.

Having problems?

If something doesn't work properly at first, don't give up.

Look through the instructions and illustrations again to see if there's anything you've missed.

Some of the activities need patience – glue takes time to set and sometimes adjustments may be needed to get something to work well.

You don't have to do the experiments in the order they are in the book, although you may find they make a little more sense if you do. You don't have to do every single one, but the more you try out, the more you will discover about forces and motion, and the more fun you will have!

Stuck for words?

If you come across a word you don't understand, or you just want to find out a bit more, have a look in the Glossary on pages 38 and 39.

Measuring forces

Forces are all around us. They are the pushes and pulls that affect something's shape and how it moves. The strength of a force is measured in newtons (N), named after the English scientist and mathematician Sir Isaac Newton. On Earth, everything has weight. This is the force of gravity pulling things downward. In everyday life, people weigh things in 'kilograms' or 'pounds'. But because weight is a force, it should really be measured in newtons. On Earth, a 100g mass has a weight of 1N, and a 1kg mass a weight of 10N.

Make a force meter

It is easy to make a force meter which you can use to measure the force of gravity.

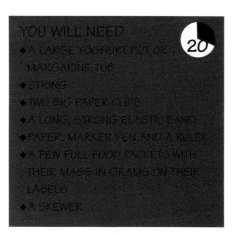

0g —
100g —
200g —
300g —
400g —
500g —

YOU WILL NEED

20

- A LARGE YOGHURT POT OR MARGARINE TUB
- STRING
- TWO BIG PAPER CLIPS
- A LONG, STRONG ELASTIC BAND
- PAPER, MARKER PEN AND A RULER
- A FEW FULL FOOD PACKETS WITH THEIR MASS IN GRAMS ON THEIR LABELS
- A SKEWER

1 Find a hook or peg somewhere, then attach a piece of paper to the wall underneath it. Loop the elastic band into a paper clip and hang the clip from the hook.

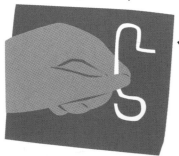

2 Open out the other paper clip to make a hook at one end and a pointer at the other. You may need some help and a pair of pliers.

3 Make holes around the rim of the pot. Use string to make a handle. Hang the pot from the elastic band with the bent paper clip.

4 Put the packets in the pot one at a time, and mark the position of the pointer each time to make a scale. Keep your eye level with the pointer. Do not overload the pot, or you will snap the elastic band! To turn your scale into newtons, remember that 100g weighs 1N, so 250g weighs 2.5N, 500g weighs 5N and so on.

What's going on?

Things have weight because gravity pulls on them. The stronger the pull of gravity on an object, the more it weighs. Weight is really the force of gravity on something. The weighing machine works because the heavier a thing is, the further it stretches the elastic band.

Newton's apple

Big discoveries are sometimes made by chance. Sir Isaac Newton was a scientist who lived in England 300 years ago. The story goes that he was sitting in his garden when he saw an apple fall from a tree. He realised that there must be an invisible force pulling the apple down towards the Earth. He wondered if this force, called gravity, might affect the Moon, the stars and the planets as well. His ideas about gravity completely changed our understanding of the Universe.

ON A DIFFERENT SCALE

It's easy to work out your weight in newtons. Just multiply your mass (in kg) by 10. On the Moon, you would only weigh one sixth as much. Mass is the same everywhere, but weight depends on where you are.

Make a weighing scale

Put the large spring or sponge into the big tin, then the smaller tin on top. Put the bag of sugar into the smaller tin. Mark the smaller tin '10N' level with the edge of the bigger tin. Use other heavy things to make a scale. You could use kitchen scales to help you do this – remember 1kg weighs 10N.

YOU WILL NEED
- TWO DEEP EMPTY CAKE TINS, ONE SMALLER THAN THE OTHER
- A LARGE SPRING FROM AN OLD MATTRESS OR CHAIR, OR A LARGE SPONGE
- A 1KG BAG OF SUGAR
- A WASHABLE MARKER PEN

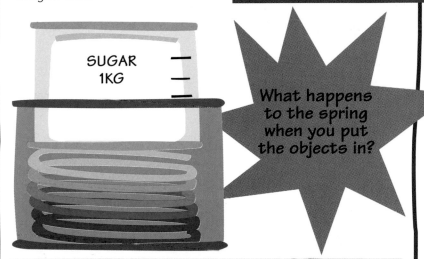

SUGAR
1KG

What happens to the spring when you put the objects in?

What's going on?

This time, instead of the force of gravity stretching an elastic band, it is squashing a spring. The more mass something has, the more strongly gravity pulls it down and the more the spring gets squashed.

Squeezing and twisting

Forces can make things change shape. Whenever something is bent, twisted, squashed or stretched a force is acting on it. Springy or elastic materials try to go back to their original shape when the force that made them change shape is taken away. This means they can store up energy and then release it to make things move. Wind-up toys and some watches work like this.

Wind-up toy

This intriguing toy shows how the energy stored in a twisted elastic band can cause movement. Ask an adult to find and break off the heads of a couple of safety matches for you.

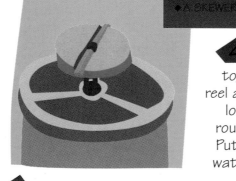

4 Wind up your toy by holding the reel and turning the long matchstick round and round. Put it down and watch it crawl!

1 Cut a thin slice from the wick end of the candle. Make the hole in the middle of the slice (where the wick was) big enough for the elastic band to fit through. Cut a groove in one side.

2 Poke the elastic band through the hole. Ask an adult for a headless matchstick, then put this through the loop and pull on the other end of the elastic band so the matchstick fits into the groove. Thread the long end of the elastic band through the reel.

3 Push half a matchstick through the loop of elastic band you have just pulled through. Stop it from turning, either with sticky tape or by wedging it with another half matchstick pushed into one of the holes in the reel.

What's going on?

As you use a turning force to twist the elastic band, you are storing up energy. Scientists call this potential energy. When you let go, the elastic band unwinds. This turns the matchstick leg and pushes the toy along. The potential energy in the twisted elastic band is turned back into movement energy.

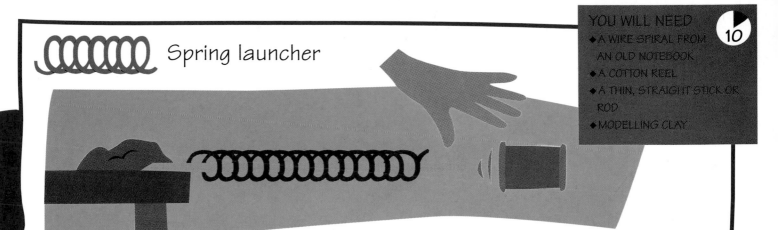

Spring launcher

YOU WILL NEED
- A WIRE SPIRAL FROM AN OLD NOTEBOOK
- A COTTON REEL
- A THIN, STRAIGHT STICK OR ROD
- MODELLING CLAY

10

Fix the stick to the edge of a table with a blob of modelling clay. Slide the spiral, and then the cotton reel, on to the stick. Press the reel down on the spiral and let go. How far can you make it fly? What happens if you give the reel more mass by sticking modelling clay to it?

What's going on?
The squashed spring pushes the reel, making it fly off the stick. The more mass the reel has, the greater the force that is needed to make it fly the same distance.

'Magic' rolling tin
Carefully make two holes in the lid and two holes in the bottom of the tin. Cut the elastic band then thread it through the holes and tie as shown. Tie on the weight where the elastic band crosses over and press the lid on. Now gently roll the tin forwards and let go.

YOU WILL NEED
- A LARGE CYLINDRICAL TIN WITH A LID
- A LONG ELASTIC BAND
- A HEAVY NUT OR SIMILAR WEIGHT
- STRING
- A HAMMER AND NAIL (ASK AN ADULT)

10

What happens when you let go of the tin?

What's going on?
The tin comes back to you because the weight stays hanging below the elastic band, making it twist when you roll the tin. It is driven along by the potential energy stored up in the twisted rubber.

WIND-UP RADIO
This portable radio never needs batteries! Instead, it has a crank which is turned by hand to store energy in a big spring. As the spring slowly unwinds, it turns a little dynamo which powers the radio for about 20 minutes at a time. It is perfect for use anywhere remote.

Gravity

Everything is attracted to everything else by the force of gravity. The attraction between everyday things is too weak to notice. We only feel gravity pulling things down towards the ground so strongly because the Earth has a lot of mass. The more mass something has, the stronger its gravitational pull. The Moon has less mass, so gravity is weaker there. Nobody is quite sure what causes gravity, but without it we would all go flying off into space!

Anti-gravity cones

You would normally expect things to roll downhill. Or would you?

YOU WILL NEED
- CARDBOARD
- TWO HALF CIRCLES OF THIN CARD
- A RULER AND PENCIL
- STICKY TAPE
- SCISSORS

10

Do the cones appear to roll uphill or downhill?

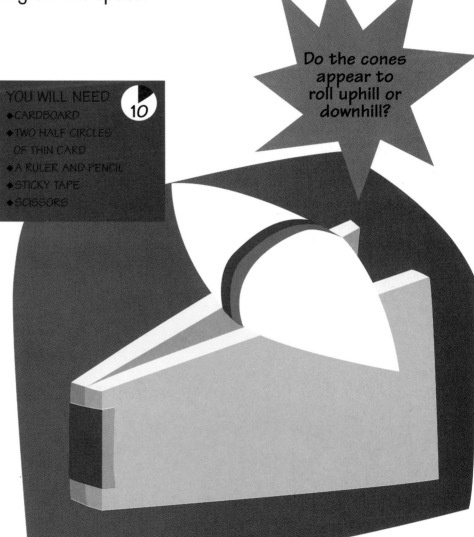

1 Cut two pieces of cardboard into the shape shown. Tape the shortest sides together. Position the two pieces as shown.

2 Roll and stick the half circles to make two matching cones. Tape the open ends together, as in the picture.

3 Put the cones at the bottom of the hill and watch them appear to defy gravity by rolling uphill!

What's going on?

The cones are not really defying gravity. They are actually going downhill. Watch the middle part carefully. Try measuring the distance from the middle of the cones to the ground at each end of the hill.

Do heavy things fall faster than light ones?

YOU WILL NEED

10

PAIRS OF THINGS THAT ARE THE SAME SIZE AND SHAPE, FOR EXAMPLE –
- A MARBLE AND A BALL BEARING
- A DICE AND A SUGAR CUBE
- A GOLF BALL AND A PING-PONG BALL
- TWO CAKE TIN LIDS OR BAKING TRAYS.

Find something safe to stand on, from which to drop your pairs of objects (a chair will do). Put the trays on the floor, one on either side of you. Drop both things from the same height at exactly the same time. Listen for them hitting the trays. Which one lands first? Try repeating your experiment to see if you get the same result every time.

Do the objects hit the trays at the same time?

What's going on?

Each pair should land together. Gravity makes them fall towards the Earth at the same rate, even though they weigh different amounts.

Galileo's story

In the 1590s, an Italian scientist called Galileo Galilei wondered if things would fall at the same speed regardless of how heavy they were. He tested his idea by dropping cannon balls of different weights from the Leaning Tower of Pisa. They always took the same time to hit the ground. His experiments got him into trouble with the Pope, who did not approve of his scientific approach to answering questions!

MOON LIGHT

This picture taken from a television transmission shows astronaut David Scott on the Moon in 1971. He took the opportunity to test Galileo's theory, this time with a feather and a hammer. There is no air on the Moon to slow down the feather, so sure enough they both hit the ground at the same time.

Balancing

Something does not have to be moving to have a force acting on it. Gravity is pulling on you now, even if you are sitting still. So what makes things fall over? Every object has a centre of gravity. This is the balancing point where the whole weight of the object seems to act. It affects how stable the object is. Things with a low centre of gravity are very stable. Things with a high centre of gravity tend to tip over.

The perching parrot

This parrot will stay on its perch, even when you try to tip it over!

YOU WILL NEED
10
◆ THICK CARD
◆ TRACING PAPER
◆ A PENCIL
◆ FELT TIP PENS
◆ SCISSORS
◆ A TABLE OR SOME STRING

1 Trace round the picture of the parrot.

2 Transfer the outline to a piece of thick card and cut it out.

3 Colour in your parrot. Perch it on the edge of a table or on a taut piece of string.

What's going on?

A lot of the parrot's mass is in its huge tail. This gives it a very low centre of gravity (actually below its feet), so it is very stable and swings back upright even when it is pushed over a little. You can get the same result by making the tail smaller, then taping a coin to each side of it to give it more mass.

Balancing potato

Try to balance a potato on the tip of your finger. Tricky! Now push two forks into the potato at an angle, one either side. Try again. No problem!

YOU WILL NEED
◆ A POTATO
◆ TWO METAL AND TWO PLASTIC FORKS

5

What happens if you try using plastic forks?

What's going on?

The mass of the forks moves the potato's centre of gravity down lower, so that it balances. This does not happen when you use light plastic forks, because they do not have enough mass.

Magic box

Tape the weight into a corner of the box and put the lid on. Slide the box over the edge of a table until only the corner with the weight in it is on the table. The rest of the box seems to be held up by thin air! If you make a false bottom to hide the weight, you can even take the lid off to show that the box is 'empty'!

YOU WILL NEED
◆ A SMALL BOX
◆ A HEAVY WEIGHT, OR SEVERAL COINS STUCK TOGETHER
◆ STICKY TAPE

5

What's going on?

A box is a regular shape, so you would expect its centre of gravity to be in the middle. Adding the weight moves the centre of gravity towards the corner. So long as the box's centre of gravity is above the table, the box will not fall off. By the way, this also explains why the Leaning Tower of Pisa (page 11) does not tip over.

BALANCING ACT
This tightrope walker is holding a long, flexible pole to lower his centre of gravity and make him more stable on the narrow rope. Even so, this act still needs plenty of practice and a good head for heights!

Pressure

You can't push your thumb into a cork. But you can easily push a drawing pin into a cork using the same force. This is because the point of the drawing pin concentrates the force on to a tiny area, causing a lot of pressure. The pressure on your thumb is much lower, because the same force is spread out over the tack's big, flat head. The more a force is spread out, the lower the pressure.

Air pressure

The force of the air pressing on things is called air pressure. Although you can't see air pressure, you can see its effect with this quick experiment.

YOU WILL NEED
- A PLASTIC TUMBLER
- A SINK
- A SHEET OF THIN, STIFF PLASTIC OR UNWANTED POSTCARD

5

1 Fill the tumbler right up to the brim with water and slide the card over the top.

2 Hold the card against the tumbler with one hand. Get hold of the tumbler with your other hand.

3 Holding the card in place, turn the tumbler upside down over the sink. Let go of the card. It should stay put, held up by nothing but air pressure!

What's going on?

Air pressure pushes in all directions, including upwards. It is easily strong enough to hold up the weight of the water in a tumbler. The card acts as a seal, keeping the air out of the tumbler as you turn it upside down. In fact, the air is pressing in on every square centimetre of your body with a force of about 10N, the same as the weight of a 1kg bag of sugar. You are not crushed because your body is pushing back with an equal, opposite force.

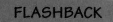
Bed of nails

In 1969, a Hindu fakir named Silki stayed on a bed of nails for 111 days. The secret of his feat is all to do with pressure. Although each single nail has a sharp point, there are hundreds of them. The total area of all those points together is enough to reduce the pressure caused by the person's weight so that the nails do not do any harm. The only tricky bit is getting on and off!

Spread the force

Try pressing a coin into a lump of modelling clay with the flat side down. Then try pressing it in with the edge down. Which is easiest?

YOU WILL NEED
◆ A COIN
◆ MODELLING CLAY
5

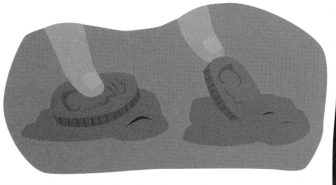

What's going on?

The coin is much easier to push in on its edge. The smaller the area, the bigger the pressure caused by the force of your hand. The face has a much bigger area than the edge of the coin, so it spreads the force out and causes a lower pressure.

TRACTOR TYRES
This tractor's huge tyres do not just help it over rough terrain. By spreading its weight over a large area, they reduce the pressure so that the tractor does not sink into the soft ground.

15

Floating and sinking

Whether something floats or sinks depends on its density. This is a way of measuring how heavy something is for its size. A steel cube, for instance, is a lot heavier than a cube of ice of the same size. The steel cube will sink in water, but the ice cube floats. We say that ice is less dense than water, in other words a cube of ice weighs less than a cube of water the same size. So far so good, but how can a steel ship stay afloat?

Deep sea diver

You can see how changing something's density makes it float or sink by making this model of a diver.

YOU WILL NEED
20
- A TWO-LITRE PLASTIC DRINKS BOTTLE (WITH LID)
- A BENDY STRAW
- A PAPER CLIP
- AN ALUMINIUM PIE TIN
- RE-USABLE ADHESIVE
- SCISSORS
- A BOWL OF WATER

4 Make diving boots out of re-usable adhesive and put them on his feet.

2 Bend the straw double, then cut it so you have a U-shaped piece about 2.5cm long. Slide the open ends of the straw on to the two ends of the paper clip.

5 Try floating your diver in a bowl of water. Carefully adjust the amount of re-usable adhesive on his boots until he just floats.

1 Cut out the shape of your diver from the pie tin. Make him tall and thin, about 7cm by 2cm, so he will fit through the neck of the bottle!

3 Gently slide the paper clip and straw between the diver's legs and up on to his body. The straw should be on his back, bent at the top behind his head, looking like a real diver's air tanks.

6 Fill the bottle with water and put the diver inside. Make sure the bottle is full to overflowing then screw the lid on tightly. The diver should float to the top.

How does a boat float?

Test your objects to see which ones float and which sink. Drop a ball of modelling clay into the water. Flatten it out and make it into a bowl shape. Will it float now? Try the same with aluminium foil.

YOU WILL NEED
- SOME SOLID OBJECTS MADE OUT OF DIFFERENT MATERIALS LIKE GLASS, METAL, WOOD AND PLASTIC
- MODELLING CLAY
- ALUMINIUM FOIL
- A LARGE BOWL OF WATER

10

How do the bowl shapes keep afloat?

What's going on?

Small, heavy things like coins and stones sink. Large, light things like corks float. But when you make a big, hollow boat shape out of something small and heavy like modelling clay, most of the boat is actually filled with air. Together, the boat and the air inside are less dense than water, so the boat floats. This is how ships can be made of steel.

7 Squeeze the bottle. The diver will sink to the bottom. Let go, and he'll float back up. With care, you can make him float at any depth you like!

What's going on?

When you squeeze the bottle, water is pushed into the straw. The air in the straw gets squeezed (compressed). This makes the diver heavier. His density increases, so he sinks. When you let go, the pressure of the air trapped in the straw pushes the water back out, making the diver less dense than water, so he floats up.

SWIMMING SHARK

Sharks are never still in the water but swim all the time. This is because they are denser than water, and if they stopped swimming they would sink.

Acceleration

Forces can make things speed up or accelerate. If the forces on something are balanced, it will not change speed. But if the force pushing an object forwards is greater than the force pushing it back, it will get faster and faster until the forces are in balance again. Unbalanced forces can make things change speed or direction.

Paddle boat

This paddle boat shows how unbalanced forces can push something forwards.

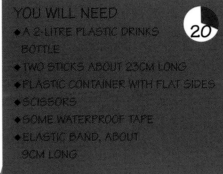

YOU WILL NEED
- A 2-LITRE PLASTIC DRINKS BOTTLE
- TWO STICKS ABOUT 23CM LONG
- PLASTIC CONTAINER WITH FLAT SIDES
- SCISSORS
- SOME WATERPROOF TAPE
- ELASTIC BAND, ABOUT 9CM LONG

20

Can you make your boat go backwards?

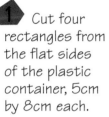

1 Cut four rectangles from the flat sides of the plastic container, 5cm by 8cm each.

2 Fold the rectangles in half and stand them on their long sides. Bring the folded edges together and secure them with tape to make a paddle.

5 Slide the paddle inside the elastic band and wind it up. Put your boat in a bath or pool of water, and let go!

3 Tape the two sticks to opposite sides of the bottle about three-quarters of the way down, so they stick out about 7cm.

4 Stretch the elastic band over the sticks. Use one that fits easily without being tightly stretched.

What's going on?

The boat is powered by the energy stored in the elastic band when you wind it up. As the paddle turns it pushes against the water, making the forces on the bottle unbalanced. It accelerates until the resistance of the water pushing back is equal to the force of the paddle pushing forwards and the forces are back in balance. Then it carries on at a steady speed until the elastic band runs out of stored energy.

Balloon boat

Soften the balloon by blowing it up a couple of times. Tape it to the straw and check that the seal is airtight. Make a small hole in one end of the tray, big enough for the straw to go through. Put the straw through the hole, blow up the balloon and seal the end of the straw with re-usable adhesive. Put the boat in some water and snip off the adhesive.

YOU WILL NEED
- A PLASTIC TRAY, THE SORT MICROWAVE MEALS COME IN
- A BENDY STRAW
- RE-USABLE ADHESIVE
- A BALLOON
- STICKY TAPE AND SCISSORS

What's going on?
The balloon pushes air out through the straw, which pushes the boat forwards. Jet engines and rockets work in just the same way, pushed forwards by gases shooting out at the back.

FLASHBACK

Land speed record
The first land speed record was set in 1898 by Count Gaston de Chasseloup-Laubat of Paris, France. His car took 57 seconds to cover a measured kilometre, averaging 63km/h. Almost 100 years later in 1997, the *Thrust SSC* supersonic car set a new record. Its twin turbojets accelerated *Thrust SSC* to an average speed of 1228km/h – faster than the speed of sound. The streamlined shape helped the car slice through the air with very little drag. Two sets of parachutes and special brakes were needed to bring it to rest.

SPRINTING CHEETAH
The cheetah holds the land speed record for animals. Its powerful legs and flexible spine allow it to accelerate to around 100km/h.

Measuring speed

Measuring speed can be very useful. Car drivers, for example, need to know if they are keeping below the speed limit. Train drivers need to know if they are going at the right speed to get to the next station at the right time. To work out how fast something is going, you need to know two things – the distance it has travelled and the time it has taken to do it.

Speed trial

Here is an easy way to measure how fast a cyclist is going. Ask an adult to find you a safe, traffic-free cycle path for this experiment.

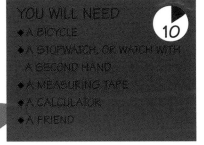

Can you work out how fast you cycle?

1 Measure the distance between two things along the side of the path (trees, for example). Try to choose things about 50m apart.

2 Take a long 'run-up' so that you are cycling at a steady speed when you pass the first post. Get your friend to time how long it takes you to travel from the first post to the second post.

$$\text{average speed} = \frac{\text{distance travelled}}{\text{time taken}}$$

What's going on?
Average speed tells you how far the cyclist goes each second. For example, if the cyclist goes 50 metres in 5 seconds, her average speed is 50/5, which is 10 metres per second or 10 m/s. Speed is often measured in kilometres per hour (kph) or miles per hour (mph), but the idea is the same.

3 Use this equation to work out how fast you were going. If you measure the distance in metres and time in seconds, the answer will be in metres per second, or m/s for short.

Balloon rocket race

Cut a few straws into 10cm lengths. Thread them on to the end of the string. Tie the string between two chairs 10m apart, pulling it tight. Blow up a balloon. Pinch the neck tightly, then get a friend to tape it to the first piece of straw. Get your stopwatch ready, and let go! Time how long the balloon takes to fly to the other end of the string. Compare different shapes of balloon to see which goes fastest.

20

Can you work out the average speed of your balloon rockets?

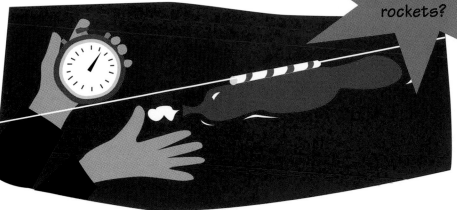

What's going on?

The balloon squeezes the air inside, forcing it out of the end. This pushes the balloon forwards. Long, thin balloons fly faster than round ones because they are a more streamlined shape and have to push less air out of the way as they go forwards.

FLASHBACK

The hare and the tortoise

In this famous ancient Greek fable, a hare challenges a tortoise to a race. The tortoise accepts, and the race begins. The hare zooms off into the distance, but then stops for a nap. Meanwhile, the tortoise plods along steadily. When the hare wakes up, the tortoise is just about to pass the winning post and the hare loses the race. Although the hare's maximum speed was far faster, his average speed over the whole race was slower than the tortoise's.

PHOTO FINISH?
When 1/100th of a second can make the difference between gold and silver, an invisible beam linked to special cameras records each runner's time more accurately than a person with a stopwatch ever could.

Friction

Whenever things rub together, friction is produced. It is an invisible force that tries to stop movement. Friction also happens when something moves through a fluid like water or air. Then it is often called 'drag'. Sometimes friction is a useful force that provides grip or slows something down, but at other times it is a nuisance. Think about a bicycle – you lubricate moving parts like the chain to reduce friction, but you would be making a big mistake to put oil on the wheel rims where the brake pads rub!

Slide or grip?

This quick experiment shows how the amount of friction between two surfaces depends on how rough or smooth they are.

YOU WILL NEED
- A LARGE WOODEN BOARD
- A SMOOTH PLASTIC TRAY
- AN ASSORTMENT OF FLAT-BOTTOMED OBJECTS THAT WON'T BREAK EASILY, EG A PLASTIC CUP, COIN, RUBBER, MATCHBOX

10

Why do some things slide more easily than others?

1 Line up your objects along one end of the wooden board. Predict which one you think will slide the easiest.

3 Now try using the plastic tray. Does it make a difference?

2 Slowly lift the end of the board and find out which thing slips the easiest, and which sticks the most.

What's going on?

Some things slide along the wooden board more easily than others because there is less friction between their bottom surface and the board. They will probably be the objects that feel smoother to the touch. Things slide much more easily along a smooth surface like the plastic tray for the same reason.

Slippery ice

Try sliding your objects along the table one by one. Now try the same with an ice cube. What do you notice?

YOU WILL NEED
◆ YOUR FLAT-BOTTOMED OBJECTS FROM 'SLIDE OR GRIP'
◆ A SMOOTH KITCHEN TABLE
◆ AN ICE CUBE

10

How can water act as a lubricant?

What's going on?

A thin layer of water from the melting ice reduces the amount of friction between the ice cube and the table, so it travels much more easily. The water acts as a lubricant, like the grease and oil between the moving parts of a machine. Water wouldn't normally be any good as a lubricant in a machine, though, because it would soon evaporate away and might make the machine parts go rusty!

Rubbing hands

Try rubbing the palms of your hands together, at first quite gently and slowly, then harder and more quickly. What do you notice? Make them wet and soapy, then try the same thing again.

YOU WILL NEED
◆ YOUR HANDS!
◆ SOAP AND WATER

5

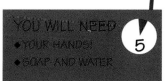

What's going on?

The harder you press your hands together and the faster you rub, the hotter they feel. This is because rubbing your hands produces friction, and friction causes heat. When you do the same thing with wet, soapy hands, the water reduces the friction and so your hands feel less hot.

ICE SKATER
The narrow blade on the skate causes very high pressure underneath. This melts the ice, making a thin layer of water which lubricates the blade just like oil. There is very little friction left to slow the skater down.

Air and water resistance

It takes a lot of effort to swim. This is because you have to push the water out of your way as you move forwards. Then there's the friction of the water sliding against your skin, and the swirling water behind you trying to pull you back. Air has the same dragging effect, but you have to go faster before you really start to notice it. Drag isn't all bad, however. If your arms and legs slid through the water without any resistance, you wouldn't be able to push yourself forwards in the first place!

Make a parachute

See how a simple parachute slows a falling object. Get an adult to help you to get the strings all the same length.

How can a parachute slow something down as it falls?

YOU WILL NEED
20
- A PLASTIC BAG
- COTTON THREAD
- SCISSORS
- A PAPER CLIP
- A HOLE PUNCH
- MODELLING CLAY TO USE AS A WEIGHT, OR A SMALL TOY TO BE YOUR PARACHUTIST

2 Tie a 40cm length of thread to each corner.

4 Drop the parachute from a safe height and see how long it takes to fall.

1 Cut out a 30cm square from the plastic bag and punch a hole close to each corner.

3 Tie the loose ends to the paper clip and add some modelling clay, or bend the paper clip to make a harness for your parachutist.

What's going on?

Parachutes work by causing as much air resistance as possible. The big, curved canopy traps air underneath which pushes up against it as it falls. The faster the parachute falls, the bigger the upwards force trying to slow it down again.

Air resistance

Stand in a space and try dropping your light objects one by one. Notice how they fall. Now get your sheets of paper tissue and screw one of them into a ball. Drop the sheet and the ball at the same time. What happens?

Why do some things fall faster than others?

What's going on?

Things speed up when you drop them, then fall at a steady speed until they reach the ground. The screwed-up paper has a smaller surface area than the sheet. It moves through the air easily, and so falls quickly. The sheet has to push a lot more air out of its way. This extra air resistance makes it float down slowly.

Water resistance

Put both the balls into the bowl of water, so that they float. Try spinning first one, and then the other. Which spins more easily?

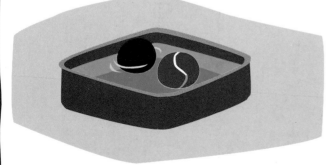

What's going on?

Water resists movement even more than air. The rubber ball spins more easily because its smooth surface does not cause as much drag as the rough tennis ball.

PARACHUTIST
When a parachute starts to fall, it accelerates until the upwards force of air resistance balances the pull of gravity. It then carries on falling at a steady speed called its 'terminal velocity'.

Floating in air

Because you cannot see it, it is easy to forget that air has weight. In fact, the atmosphere weighs a lot – try the air pressure experiment on page 14. Just like water, air causes an upwards force on things, called 'upthrust'. Believe it or not, if you put a weight on some scales and then take the air away, it will weigh more, in the same way that you weigh more when you let the water out of your bath. Something will float in air, just as in water, if the upthrust on it is equal to or more than its weight.

Make a hot air balloon

This balloon is quite tricky to make, but loads of fun! Ask an adult for help. Once you have made a working model you can scale it up to make a really big one.

YOU WILL NEED
- SHEETS OF TISSUE PAPER
- SCISSORS
- GLUE
- A HAIRDRYER
- BENDY STRAWS

20

1 Make a template, and then cut out eight pieces of tissue paper in the shape shown.

2 Using as little glue as you can, stick the edges together to make a balloon shape. It does not matter if you have to scrunch up the tissue a little to get it into the right shape, as long as there are no gaps left along the joins. A round patch of tissue will seal any gaps at the top.

3 Ask an adult to fill the balloon with hot air using the hairdryer. If it flips upside down, strengthen the hole by sticking in some bendy straws around the opening.

What makes your balloon fly?

What's going on?

Heating the air inside the balloon makes the air expand, pushing some out of the bottom. Now less air is taking up the same space, so it is less dense. The upthrust caused by the cooler, heavier air around the balloon makes it float upwards. As it cools down, the air in the balloon gets denser and heavier again, so the balloon comes down.

Hovering helium

Make lots of identical weights by cutting up aluminium trays into, say, squares 2cm x 2cm. Using a straightened paper clip, carefully poke a hole through one corner of each weight. Tie a paper clip to the helium balloon with string, and bend it to make a hanger for your aluminium weights. Attach weights one at a time until the balloon can only just lift them. Every hour or so you will have to take some weights off to keep the balloon in the air.

What's going on?

Air is a mixture of gases, mostly nitrogen and oxygen, which are heavier than helium, which is a very light gas. A helium-filled balloon is lighter than air and floats upwards. The molecules of helium are so tiny, though, that after a while they start to leak out. The shrinking balloon gets heavier than air and gravity pulls it back down.

FLASHBACK

The deck chair pilot

In 1982 one-time pilot Larry Walters decided to fly once more. He tied 45 helium-filled weather balloons to a garden chair and took off, hoping to float just above the ground. Instead, he shot into the sky to a height of 3,200m. After 14 cold, terrifying hours he drifted past an airliner, whose pilot reported seeing a man on a garden chair at 3,000m! Mr Walters was blown out to sea where he was finally rescued by a helicopter, which towed him to safety.

A HOT AIR BALLOON
A powerful burner heats the air inside the balloon. The cooler, denser air outside the balloon causes upthrust, lifting the balloon skywards. Regular blasts of heat will be needed to keep the balloon floating in the air.

Flight

There are other ways to create upwards forces on things to make them fly, apart from using hot air or a light gas like helium. Birds and flying insects use flapping wings to give them lift, pushing the air down and backwards to move forwards through the air. Aeroplanes use the same idea, but have fixed wings and propellers or jet engines to push them forwards. The lift comes from the shape of the wings. Rockets work by blasting hot gases from the tail which push the rocket forwards, even in the airless vacuum of space.

Make a rocket

This water rocket is great fun, but you will need an adult to help make it and supervise the launch.

YOU WILL NEED
- A PLASTIC SOFT DRINKS BOTTLE
- A CORK OR BUNG THAT FITS THE BOTTLE
- BALSA WOOD AND STRONG GLUE
- A DRILL WITH A SMALL BIT (ASK AN ADULT)
- A BICYCLE PUMP WITH CONNECTOR
- A NEEDLE ADAPTOR (THE SORT USED TO BLOW UP BASKETBALLS AND FOOTBALLS)
- GLUE

1 Cut three or four fins out of balsa wood in the shape shown and glue them to the bottle. The rocket should be able to stand on its fins. Let the glue set.

3 Fill the bottle about a quarter full with water and push the cork in hard.

2 Ask an adult to drill a small hole through the cork and push the needle adaptor in from the wide end. It needs to be a tight fit.

4 Take your rocket into the middle of an open space like a playing field, far away from buildings or overhead wires. Attach the connector and bicycle pump. Pump air into the bottle, keeping well back. Pressure will build up until the cork pops out and the rocket blasts off!

Make a glider

Follow the diagrams to fold the paper. Add a paper clip to the nose, then throw your glider gently. Experiment by moving the paper clip to see which position makes the glider fly the furthest.

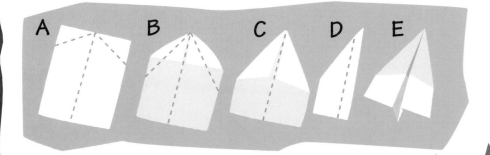

A   B   C   D   E

What's going on?
The glider flies a long way because of air resistance pushing up against the flat wings, opposing the pull of gravity.

Make a gyrocopter

Draw out the shape shown. Cut the side strips and fold them out to make the wings. Attach a paper clip to the bottom of your gyrocopter, then throw it up into the air.

What happens if you make one twice as big?

What's going on?
A gyrocopter is a helicopter without a motor. Air resistance causes the wings to spin as it falls. The spinning wings create lift which works in the opposite direction to gravity, slowing down its fall. Sycamore trees use the same trick to spread their seeds. The bigger the gyrocopter, the slower it falls.

What's going on?
Pumping air into the bottle increases the pressure inside until it overcomes the friction holding the cork in the neck of the bottle. The air and water blasting out of the bottom causes a reaction force which pushes the rocket upwards into the sky.

CRUISING CONDOR
Birds are masters of flight. Condors like this one flap their wings to take off and gain height. They can then glide for long distances. The shape of their wings gives them lift, and they can ride on rising columns of warmer air, called thermals, for hours.

Force magnifiers

Levers and pulleys are 'force magnifiers'. How would you get the lid off a can of paint? You could use a screwdriver or something similar as a lever. Think about a door handle. You push the handle a long way to make the latch move only a little to open the door. These are 'force magnifiers'. A small force is used to move one end a long way, causing a big force to move something a short distance at the other end.

Pulley power

Delight your friends and worry your enemies with this demonstration of your superhuman strength!

YOU WILL NEED
- TWO BROOMS OR MOPS
- A FEW METRES OF ROPE
- SOME TALC
- A FEW FRIENDS

10

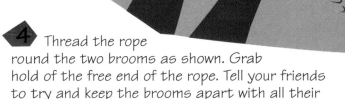

1 Tie the rope near the end of one broom.

2 Dust the two broom handles with talcum powder to reduce friction.

3 Get two or even four friends to hold the two brooms apart.

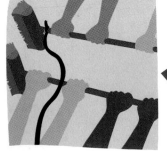

4 Thread the rope round the two brooms as shown. Grab hold of the free end of the rope. Tell your friends to try and keep the brooms apart with all their strength while you effortlessly pull them together!

What's going on?

Because of the way the rope is threaded between the brooms, pulling the free end a long way with a small force causes a huge force to tug the brooms a little way together. The broom handles are acting like pulleys. The more times the rope loops back and forth, the greater the force magnifying effect.

Make a double pulley

Ask an adult to cut a coat hanger into two pieces and bend them to hold the cotton reels and toy bucket as shown. Hang the wire without the bucket from a hook, attach the string as shown then thread it round all the pulleys. Try lifting some weights with your double pulley.

YOU WILL NEED
◆ FOUR COTTON REELS
◆ A WIRE COAT HANGER
◆ STRING
◆ A TOY BUCKET AND SOME THINGS TO PUT IN IT
◆ WIRE CUTTERS

20

How can you lift the bucket using the double pulley?

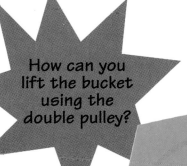

What's going on?
The double pulley works just like the broom trick. Pulling the string a long way with a small force lifts the weight a little way with a big force, so the bucket is easy to lift.

Levers

Ask an adult to bang the lid on to the tin so that it's really tight. Try levering it off, first with the handle of a teaspoon then with the dessert spoon handle. Take care not to bend the spoons!

YOU WILL NEED
◆ A TIN WITH A TIGHT LID, LIKE A COCOA TIN
◆ A TEASPOON
◆ A DESSERT SPOON

5

What's going on?
The longer a lever is, the greater the turning force it can cause. The spoon handle is the lever and the rim of the tin is the pivot. When you press on the spoon, your hand moves a long way with a small force. The end of the handle pushes the lid up a small way with a big force.

LOAD LIFTER
A wheelbarrow is a force magnifier. The wheel is the pivot and the handles are the lever. By lifting the handles a long distance with a small force, you can lift a heavy load just off the ground with a big force.

Gears

Gears are wheels with teeth round the outside. They can be connected directly together or joined by a chain. Depending on the sizes of the gear wheels, gears can be used as force magnifiers or movement magnifiers. They are used in all sorts of machines to change the speed or direction of movement. Bicycles and cars need gears to cope with going up and down hills and travelling at different speeds.

Bicycle gears

This experiment will show you the effect that gears have on a bicycle's movement.

1 Put the bicycle into its lowest gear.

2 Make a chalk mark on the path next to the back wheel, where it touches the ground.

3 Gently turn the pedals once, walking the bicycle forwards in a straight line. Make a second mark next to the back wheel. Measure the distance between the marks.

How do bicycle gears work?

4 Put the bicycle into top gear and repeat the experiment. How far does it go this time?

What's going on?

Bottom gear works as a force magnifier. It is very slow on flat ground, but good for climbing hills. The pedals go round quickly compared to the wheel. Top gear is for pedalling downhill or going fast on the level. The wheel goes round quickly compared to the pedals, but with much less power.

Making gears

Mark the centre of each lid and ask an adult to punch a hole through. Glue a cotton reel on to each lid in line with the hole. Stretch a thick elastic band round the rim of each lid to give them grip. Push two nails through the card, spaced so that when you slot two lids over them their rims just touch. Turn the larger lid and see how the smaller lid moves. Try some different combinations of lid sizes – you could even arrange three lids in a row. You will have to move the nails each time you change lid.

YOU WILL NEED
◆ WIDE ELASTIC BANDS
◆ THICK CARD
◆ A HAMMER AND TWO 4CM NAILS
◆ COTTON REELS
◆ JAR LIDS OF VARIOUS SIZES

20

What's going on?

This is just like the top gear on a bicycle, only without the chain to link the two gear wheels. Turning the large wheel slowly makes the small wheel spin quickly, without much force, in the opposite direction. You can change it into a model of bottom gear by using the small wheel to turn the larger wheel. Now the big wheel turns slowly with a lot of force.

FLASHBACK

Harrison's chronometer

Gears are not only useful on big machines like bicycles. The mechanism of a clock uses precision gears to steadily turn the hands at exactly the right speed. The first really reliable portable clock, the H4 chronometer, was built nearly 250 years ago by English watchmaker John Harrison. With its intricate mechanism of gears and springs, H4 could keep good time, even on a ship at sea. This was a huge breakthrough. By keeping accurate track of the time, sailors could work out their precise position. It took Harrison 40 years to develop the H4, but it was worth it as he was awarded £18,000 for his achievement.

SPEED BIKE
Chris Boardman won Olympic gold in 1992 riding this very light superbike. The chainring cog is much bigger than the cog on the back wheel, giving very high gearing. The bike and rider have a streamlined shape, helping them to glide easily through the air.

Circular motion

Anything spinning around has circular motion. Remember that moving things will always go in a straight line unless there is a force tugging them off course. When something moves in a circle, it is constantly changing direction. For this to happen, there has to be a force pulling it towards the middle of the circle. Scientists call this centripetal force. You can easily feel this force on a playground roundabout, tugging on your arms as your body tries to fly off in a straight line!

Spinning force

This experiment shows how centripetal force increases the faster something spins round. Find a space away from anyone else to do this!

YOU WILL NEED
- A CORK OR RUBBER BUNG
- ABOUT 1M OF STRING
- A COTTON REEL
- A SMALL WEIGHT, LIKE A WOODEN BLOCK
- A DRILL (ASK AN ADULT)

10

What happens to the weight when the cork whirls round?

1 Ask an adult to drill a small hole lengthwise through the cork.

2 Thread one end of the string through the cork and tie a big enough knot in the end to stop the cork sliding off.

4 Hold the cotton reel. Start whirling the cork round in a circle, slowly at first and then faster and faster.

3 Thread the other end of the string through the cotton reel and tie it to the weight.

What's going on?

As the cork spins faster, the centripetal force needed to keep it going round in a circle instead of flying off in a straight line increases. This force tugs on the string, lifting the weight up. The faster you spin the cork, the higher the weight is lifted.

Make a spinner

Draw a circle on the card and cut it out. Carefully push the pointed end of a pencil through the centre of the circle. Spin the pencil on a smooth, flat surface.

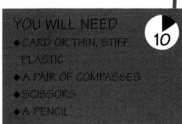
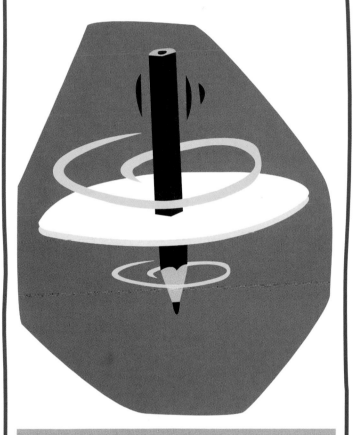

What's going on?
Spinning objects like wheels and gyroscopes resist being tilted. This makes them very stable. The spinner will make the pencil balance on its point, especially if the centre of gravity is kept low by having the card low down on the pencil.

A FAIRGROUND RIDE
Spinning fairground rides work by upsetting your sense of gravity. This one spins you round, like the bucket of water, so that you can't tell up from down. Your body is trying to fly off in a straight line, but the ride is pulling you round and round in a circle.

Anti-gravity water

Tie the string to the bucket's handle. Half fill the bucket with water. Hold the string and lift the bucket so that it hangs just above the ground. Start turning round, very slowly at first, then spin faster and faster. Watch what happens to the water as the bucket moves up higher.

What's going on?
Centripetal force affects liquids, too. As the bucket spins, the water is trying to go in a straight line. The bottom of the bucket keeps pushing the water in towards the middle of the circle and the water gets pressed against the bottom of the bucket, so it can't spill out. The water stays inside the bucket, even when the bucket is on its side!

Starting and stopping

It takes a push or a pull to start something moving or to make it stop. Imagine pushing a heavy shopping trolley. You have to push hard to start it moving, but once you've got it going it will keep going by itself even if you let go. You have to pull back on the handle to make it stop. This tendency of things to keep still if they're still, or keep moving if they're already moving, is called inertia. The more mass something has, the greater its inertia.

Don't lose your marbles

This simple experiment shows how inertia affects the motion of some marbles in a shoe box lid. You will need to use a smooth level floor.

YOU WILL NEED
- A FEW MARBLES OF VARIOUS SIZES
- A SHOE BOX LID
- STICKY TAPE
- A SKATEBOARD OR TOY WITH WHEELS

10

4 Watch the marbles as you stop the skateboard by pulling back on it.

1 Use tape to stick the lid firmly to the top of the skateboard and put it on the floor.

What happens if the skateboard stops suddenly?

2 Position the marbles in the lid so they are spaced apart from one another.

3 Start the skateboard moving by pushing it gently. Watch carefully what happens to the marbles.

What's going on?

Because they have inertia, the marbles try to stay still as you push the skateboard forwards. They only start moving when the back wall of the lid gives them a push. When the skateboard stops, they try to carry on moving forwards and roll to the front of the lid. The heavier the marble is, the more inertia it has and the more it resists any change in its motion.

Spinning egg puzzle

You can use this trick of inertia to find out if an egg is raw or cooked. Spin the cooked egg and then stop it spinning by gently grabbing it. Let go straight away. It will stop, like you would expect. Try the same with the raw egg. After you've stopped it and let go, it starts spinning again!

What's going on?

The liquid inside the raw egg has inertia and carries on swirling around inside when you grab the shell. When you let go, the whole egg starts spinning again.

Demolish the tower

Build a tower of draughts near the edge of a smooth table. Put a ruler on the table next to the tower with one end sticking out past the end of the table. Holding this end, slice the ruler quickly through the bottom of the tower by sliding it along the table with a flicking motion. With practice, you should be able to knock out the bottom draught one by one without toppling the tower.

What's going on?

The quick push needed to knock the bottom draught out is too small a force to overcome the inertia of the whole tower, which stays put. The magician's trick of whipping the tablecloth out from under some plates and glasses relies on inertia in the same way.

BELT UP!
These inertia-reel seatbelts unwind easily when you pull gently to put them on. If the car stops suddenly, for example in an accident, the children's inertia will keep them moving forwards. This tugs quickly on the seatbelts, which instantly lock and hold the children safely in their seats.

Glossary

Acceleration   When an object changes its speed or direction, it is accelerating. Acceleration is measured in metres per second squared (m/s^2).

Air pressure   The pressure caused by the weight of the atmosphere, also called atmospheric pressure. Although it is invisible, air has mass, so it is pulled down by the Earth's gravity. The pressure of the air at the Earth's surface is about ten newtons per square centimetre ($10N/cm^2$). Weather maps show areas of higher or lower air pressure, as these have a strong effect on the weather.

Air resistance   The resistance of air to the motion of objects travelling through it. This resistance happens because moving objects rub against the molecules of the gases that make up the air.

Balanced forces   Forces that do not cause any change in the motion of an object when they interact are said to be balanced. When you sit on a chair, for example, the force of gravity pulling you down is balanced by the equal and opposite reaction force of the chair pushing you up.

Centre of gravity (or centre of mass)   The point in an object where the force of gravity appears to act. If it is suspended from any point on the vertical line passing through its centre of gravity, the object will stay balanced.

Centripetal force   The force that causes something to move in a circular path. When you twirl a stone around on a string, you have to pull on the string to keep the stone from flying off in a straight line. The force of the string tugging on the stone is the centripetal force.

Density   How much mass something has in relation to its volume. Density is worked out by dividing a substance's mass by its volume, measured in grams per centimetre cubed (g/cm^3).

Drag   An aerodynamic force that resists the forward motion of an object. The shape of the object affects the amount of drag.

Energy   The ability to do work. Work is done whenever a force moves through a distance, so you can think of energy as a 'promise' to do work. There are several kinds of energy, like light, heat, electrical energy and potential energy. Both work and energy are measured in joules (J).

Force magnifier   A machine where a small force moving a long distance causes a big force to move a small distance, for example a door handle.

Forces   The pushes or pulls that can change something's speed, shape or direction. Forces are measured in newtons (N).

Friction   The rubbing force that resists movement when things slide against each other.

Gears   Toothed wheels used in machines to make one wheel turn another.

Gravitational pull   The pull of one object on another due to the force of gravity. For example, the Earth's gravity keeps satellites in orbit.

Gravity   A force of attraction that pulls everything towards everything else. The strength of attraction depends on the mass of the objects and how far apart they are.

Inertia   The tendency of any object to stay still or move steadily in a straight line unless a force makes it do otherwise. The more mass something has, the greater its inertia.

Kilogram   The standard unit of mass. A volume of one litre of water has a mass of one kilogram.

Lever   A rigid bar that can turn on a pivot or hinge to transmit a force from one place to another. Wheelbarrows, scissors and the muscles and joints of your body are all examples of lever systems.

Lift   An aerodynamic force caused by the motion of a wing through the air. Lift allows an aeroplane to climb into the air and holds it up during flight.

Lubricant   A substance that reduces the friction between two surfaces.

Machine   A device that does work. Machines are designed to make life easier for us.

Mass   The amount of material an object contains.

Motion   Motion occurs when something changes its position.

Movement magnifier   A mechanism where a large force moving a short distance causes a small force to move a long distance, for example the pedal that opens the lid of a pedal bin.

Newton   Unit for measuring forces. The pull of Earth's gravity on a mass of 1kg is almost exactly 10N.

Potential energy   Energy that is stored. When you lift something up or stretch a spring, you give it potential energy.

Pressure   How concentrated or spread out a force is over a surface. Pressure is calculated by dividing the size of the force by the area it is acting on. It is measured in pascals (Pa) or newtons per square metre (N/m^2).

Pulley   A wheel with a grooved rim. Several can be used together to make it easier to lift a heavy load. This is an example of a force magnifier.

Speed   How fast something is going. Speed is calculated by dividing distance by time. Average speed is the total distance travelled on a journey divided by the total time taken.

Streamlined   A shape which reduces drag. A fish has a streamlined shape.

Turning force   The strength of a turning effect. The longer a lever, the greater the turning force it can produce. Also called a 'moment'.

Unbalanced forces   Forces that cause a change in the motion or shape of an object, because the force acting in one direction is greater than the force acting in the opposite direction.

Upthrust   The upwards force that acts on an object when it is immersed in a fluid. The size of the force is the same as the weight of the fluid that makes way for the object.

Weight   The force of gravity pulling on a mass on or near the surface of a planet. On Earth, a mass of one kilogram weighs 9.8 newtons.

Index

A B C

Balancing 12, 13
Bed of nails 15
Bicycle 20, 32, 33
Bird 29
Boardman, Chris 33
Boat 17, 18, 19
Cheetah 19
Clock 33

D E

Density 16, 17, 26
Diver 16, 17
Drag 19, 22, 24
Elastic 8
Energy
   movement 8
   potential 8, 9,18

F

Flight
   glider 29
   gyrocopter 29
   jet 19, 28
   lift 28, 29
   rocket 19, 21, 28
Floating 16, 17, 26, 27
Forces
   balanced 18
   centripetal 34, 35
   force magnifiers 30, 31, 32
   force meter 6
   friction 22, 23, 24, 30
   measuring of 6
   newtons 6, 7
   unbalanced 18
   upthrust 26, 27
   weight 6

G H

Galilei, Galileo 11
Gears 32, 33
Gravity

centre of 12, 13, 35
   force of 6, 7, 10, 11, 35
Gyroscope 35
Harrison, John 33
Helium 27
Hot air balloon 26, 27

I J K

Inertia 36, 37
Kilograms 6

L

Land speed record 19
Levers 31
Lubricant 23

M N O

Mass 7, 9, 10, 12, 13, 36
Moon 7, 10, 11
Motion
   acceleration 18, 19
   average speed 20, 21
   circular 34, 35
   measuring speed 20, 21
   movement magnifiers 32
Newton, Isaac 7

P

Parachute 24, 25
Pisa, Leaning Tower of 11
Pressure 14, 15, 23, 28, 29
Pulleys 30, 31

Q R

Resistance
   air 24, 25, 29
   water 18, 24, 25

S

Scott, David 11
Seat belts 37
Shark 17

Silki 15
Skater, ice 23
Spinner 35
Streamlining 19, 21, 33

T U V

Terminal velocity 25
Tightrope walker 13
Tractor 14

W X Y Z

Walters, Larry 27
Weighing scale 7
Wheelbarrow 31
Wind-up radio 9

Picture Credits

Telegraph Colour Library (bottom right) 7, 13, 37

Freeplay Energy (bottom right) 9

NASA (bottom right) 11

Rex Features Ltd (bottom right) 15, 25

Gettyone Stone (bottom right) 17, 19, 27

Empics (bottom right) 21, 23, 33

Bruce Coleman Collection (bottom right) 29

Arena Images (bottom right) 35

Image Bank (bottom right) 31